LIFE
Cycles

Journeys of an Accidental Poet

MICHAEL REINSEL

Copyright © 2021 Michael Reinsel
All Rights Reserved

Year of the Book
135 Glen Avenue
Glen Rock, PA 17327

Print ISBN: 978-1-64649-208-4
Ebook ISBN: 978-1-64649-209-1

This book or parts thereof may not be reproduced in any form, stored in any retrieval system, or transmitted in any form by any means—electronic, mechanical, photocopy, recording, or otherwise—without prior written permission of the publisher, except as provided by United States of America copyright law.

The following poems have previously appeared in *Reflections Magazine*, Notre Dame of Maryland University:

    "Bellona Avenue Descent" (2014-2015)
    "Among the Amish" (2015-2016)
    "Erratics" (2016-2017)
    "Flattened Pennies" (2017-2018)
    "Lost Again" (2018-2019)
    "Found a Pen" (2019-2020)
    "In Another Life" (2020-2021)

Cover Photo by the author.

DEDICATION

To Evie—for everything

Contents

I. NATURE/TRAVEL

Dressing for the Ball 3
Trail Signs 4
Hedera Helix 6
A Fox, Buck, and Butterfly 8
The Catbird and Me 9
An Old Friend 10
Lunch 12
Hard Times 14
Mobile Home 16
Seven Days 18
Traditions 20
Outside Life 21
Silence 22
Décor 23
Just Passing Through 24
Heartbeats 26
To Touch 27
Sunset 28
Beyond Time 29
Shoveling Snow 30
Missing the Snow 32
Pining 33
An Extra Blanket in April 34
Buffalo Bull Sits Down 36
Thoreau's Favorite 38
A Dying Art 39
American Hero 40
Suomi Whispers 42
Erratics 43
Treverien 44

II. CYCLING

Lost Again 49
Bellona Avenue Descent 50
Red Epaulettes 51
Montebello 52
Heroes 54
March Ride 56
Aprilis 57
The Route Matters 59
Under the Covid Sky 61
Among the Amish 63
Crossing the Road 65
Lost 66
Earthbound 69
Oasis 70
Harvest 72
The Death Still Haunts Him 74
Requiem for a Possum 75
January Pedaling 76
For the Birds 77
Trail Friends 78

III. GRANDCHILDREN

Weightless 81
Breaking Bread at Springlake 82
An Exotic Gem 84
First Things 86
Learning and Teaching 88
Did *You* Know? 90
Chickadee 92
Family Tree 94
Driving with Colin 95
Behind the Garage 96
Pleyen 98
How Many Days 100

Playing with a Golden Shovel 102
Skipping with Zach and the Gerrids 103
Touched by Nature 104
A Smile Says It All 106
The Quietest Day 108
Something About 110
Always Be..111

IV. FAMILY
Distant Kin... 115
Hope 118
Flattened Pennies 119
Going Home.. 120
Wooden Nickels 122
This Quiet Place 124
H-O-M-E 126
Waiting 128
A Love for All 130
Happy Birthday 131
Wearing Green...132
Bitten 134
Something Great...136
A Day in the Life 138
Waiting for Dad 139
Walking with My Father.. 140

V. AGING/ART
Life in Small Words 145
Antiques..147
Aging in Place 148
Amalgam 150
Gravitas...151
Given Time 152
Communion 154
Identity 156
Indebted to Pheidippides 158

Frank's Gift 160
Among Friends 162
Only...163
Found a Pen...164
Everyday Artists 165
I Should Have Been 166
The Hardest Part 168
If Only I Had Known 170
Living in the Shadow 172
The Poet Within..174
The Poet Next Door 176
Playing Catch 177
In Another Life 178

I

NATURE / TRAVEL

I've always felt more at home in nature than anywhere else. Growing up surrounded by nature was a precious gift. In nature, experiences uncover memories that unfold on the page. Boy Scouts kindled my love of adventure and nature.

Growing up in a small village planted the seed of wanderlust in me. Seeing new places, often on a bicycle, means receiving the kindness of strangers on a daily basis—a gift you never forget. My first cycle tour in 1984—solo camping around Nova Scotia from Maine—was an amazing journey that lit the flame. My first trip to Europe—hitchhiking around England, Scotland, and Ireland in 1985—cemented travel into my consciousness. Home is often best appreciated through the lens of travel.

Dressing for the Ball

the cardinal sings Caruso from the budding maple
daffodils linger in the lawn shyly waving to all
forsythia sunshine illuminates a gray Spring day
lilacs slowly get dressed, looking for their perfume

daffodils linger in the lawn shyly waving to all
a weed by any other name, a dandelion smiles
lilacs slowly get dressed, looking for their perfume
the dogwood begins to put on its creamy petticoat

a weed by any other name, a dandelion smiles
skunk cabbage cavorts before the wood dons its green
the dogwood begins to put on its creamy petticoat
tulips rise as wild garlic stands tall, mingling in clusters

skunk cabbage cavorts before the wood dons its green
azaleas awaken and hope they will be dressed in time
forsythia sunshine illuminates a gray Spring day
the cardinal sings Caruso from the budding maple

April 2015

Trail Signs

mid-summer walk down woodbrook lane
gravity's pull under full sun
few grand estates still call this home
once rural now an enclosed nook
tyrconnell always draws me in
stone wall iron gate towering oaks
far from ireland yet not so far
blacktop road ends dirt trail begins
footprints of those who trod before

bird sings reveille high above
sign says entering lake roland
old name was robert e lee park
historic names are now changing
poison ivy's fangs creep trailside
beer pull-tab rises from the dirt
bright green plastic flossing device
garbage fossils from modern man
must gingivitis be felt here

wave to others on the same trail
our masks make speaking difficult
initials carved in big gray beech
old scars from hormones dead and gone
broken glass amidst brick fragments
from days when cars could pass this way
blackberries yet engulfed in fuzz
dragonfly hovers beside me
there is still magic in nature

bottle top soda can dog doo
who would deface this living space
fishermen stand along the shore
water rushes over the dam
pulling my spirit down the stream
still waters speak as they spill forth
restroom sign   closed covid-19
trail signs arise in many forms
trail signs are not meant to explain

June 2020

Hedera Helix

Dark green English ivy clung tightly
to the gray trunks of oak and maple
climbing skyward, ever higher
unaware that it was slowly killing
its tall old friend to whom it
has been so attached for years.
Hedera Helix is its formal name
the first means ivy and the last
name is ancient Greek for twist, turn

Ivy was sacred to the God Dionysus
He was fathered by Zeus, king of the gods
in an affair with his mother Semele,
a mortal who perished viewing Zeus
The deity saved the unborn baby
by sewing him into his thigh
so that Dionysus could be born
full-grown from his leg on Ikaria.

With such divine roots
this aristocratic vine
its bloodlines so fine
seems to belong to the bricks
it slowly and steadily climbs
skyward looking for Dionysus
a living sculpture, centipedian
tiny brown tentacles clawing
brick, bark, wood, siding or earth
always looking for untouched
places to invade and conquer
spreading into green ivy deserts

Will future generations be pulling
and cutting this kudzu-like predator
that often appears as part of a still life
when gazed upon out the back window
rising from the snow to climb the fence
determined to make it into the next yard
like a prehistoric creature that
seems destined to outlive us
perhaps a name change is called for
would Russian Ivy be taken more seriously?

March 2015

A Fox, Buck, and Butterfly

all within my sight did lie
was this a sign from on high
or just coincidence said I
nature's eyes gazed into mine
tiger swallowtail's wings belie
the stillness that is nigh
fox in royal red so sly
buck wearing his crown so high
do keep watch for by and by
beauty comes to those who try

maybe I will never spy
a fox, buck and butterfly
all looking me in the eye
but that won't make me sigh
beauty lives in memory
on the page or in a tree
life is not meant to flee
life is all in how you see

a fox, buck, and butterfly
all within my sight did lie
enchanting scenes there may be
this one means the world to me

October 2020

The Catbird and Me

the catbird is great company
greets me in the yard with a song
in this beautiful month of may
where I'm to be found most days now
because the virus lurks about
distancing in place soon gets old
these days there are no catbird seats

making a new friend is fun
especially when they can sing
catbird is my caruso
sounds belie that sleek gray body
so full of cheer and melody
mimicking is his specialty
other birds wonder who is he

catbird visits every evening
arrives when I need him most
sings as I patch holes in the lawn
dug up by those furry gray rodents
in search of their misplaced acorns
catbird's solos always soothe me
these backyard arias—priceless

it is early December now
catbird has been gone for awhile
took off one night for Florida
seems goodbyes must be hard for him
our backyard is ghostly silent
bare trees shiver in the cold breeze
I feel another year older

December 2020

An Old Friend

our vacation is over
an old friend awaits
three glorious weeks
the reluctant drive home
my old friend looks ragged
frayed by July's heat
jealous of our trip north
cooler temps must be nice
no way he could leave home
browned by summer's sun
his bare spots stand out
for twenty-six years
we've touched base each day
except when I'm away

quiet day in august
a cardinal sings alone
where are the other birds
common pokeweed towers
over the old chain link
plump berries purpling
daylilies came and went
hydrangeas green not blue
anything for some shade
cicada sounds abound
morning glories climb
over all they can reach
iris blades flowerless
lilacs shed their leaves
bird nests are all vacant
two white moths float by
playing tag in warm air
while crickets count time

black-eyed susans shine
through the august heat
a lone bed of beauty
within our weary gaze
hope my old friend the yard
soon sees better days
how about some water

August 2019

LUNCH

I didn't know you were near
as I sit down in the tall grass
beneath the old campus oak
kindly muting the autumn sun
open my knapsack for lunch
you suddenly catch my eye
no doubt you saw me first
through those big green eyes
your emerald outfit blending
as one with the grass blades
silently our eyes meet
sharing a moment
caressed by the soft breeze
fleeting shadows bewitch

I say hello
you only nod
your lithe limbs stretch
each move a ballet
you watch me eat
sliced apple PB&J
not sure if you've eaten
I offer you the apple
but your mind is set
on something fresher still
I've admired you from afar
our closeness gives me a thrill
slender torso strong legs broad back
an enchanting heart-shaped face
living a still life in this place

next thing I know
you are walking away
not even a goodbye
only a glance my way
long legs climbing down and up
over the tall grass blades
away from our quiet spot
together under the campus oak
I won't forget you
Mantis—pray for me

October 2017

Hard Times

Sitting in a cramped seat
between silent strangers
six hours without a word
must be the norm these days
devices do the talking
humans watch and listen
pixels and digital sounds
keep the masses entranced

Dickens is my salvation
words on the printed page
nineteenth century stuff
Hard Times tugs at me
in this cramped hard seat
my aching back feels for Louisa
as she rebels from her father
Gradgrind teaches only facts

Bounderby's bluster repels
those whose mortal toil tolls
within Coketown's smoky mills
while Mrs. Sparsit ingratiates
brother Tom falls deeper into debt
Stephen's luck turns bad to worse
Rachael is his reason to live
Sissy's a gift from the circus

not sure I'd have survived
without Hard Times in my hands
the loud hiss of the jet plane
punctuated by headphone noise
one hundred fifty people
five hundred miles an hour
six miles above terra firma
flying east to west

facts never reveal
the entire story
nobody ever makes it
entirely on their own
we all need
another's help
perhaps next time
I will speak first

March 2019

Mobile Home

The brown and yellow carapace
appears as if by magic
at the base of the old maple
whose roots fan out
beneath my domed green tent
like strong gray fingers
deeply clawing the earth

these same long hard fingers
dig into my aging back
as I roll over in the night
vainly trying to find sleep
on the slanted hard ground
while raindrops tap the tent
I futilely attempt
to disregard nature's call

I resist the consuming urge
to pick up the box turtle
a kaleidoscope of color
that would fit perfectly
into my outstretched palm
but instead stand quietly
watching it watch me

looking over at my wet tent
waiting to be packed up
on this gloomy October morning
I envied its tiny house
a flawless mobile home
matching the brown and yellow leaves
with no other place else to be

after my first soggy trip to the car
it was on the other side of the tree
standing still on some moss
looking completely prehistoric
red eyes and yellow-scaled legs
ready for a Sunday morning stroll
after my next load it was gone
wish I could have come along
been thinking about downsizing

October 2017

Seven Days

of splitting wood
staring into glowing embers
gazing upon tall pines
watching the river flow
waking under the cool fog
talking to chipmunks
watching the reds and yellows
autumn slowly appears
admiring the regal
stride of wild turkeys
listening to crickets
chirp an end to summer

reverently hiking
among the old growth
hidden from the sun
beneath centuries old
beech hemlock white pine
petting moss-covered boulders
smelling the fresh scent
of fern-laden air

paddling downstream
among the rocks and eddy's
canoe scraping in the shallows
pedaling beside the river
past perfect campsites
and giant rhododendron
more caterpillars than cars
breathing in the river
like the Iroquois
who trod this Catawba path
for thousands of years

seven days of September
in the autumn of life
returning to this wild place
where identity took root
and dreams unfurled
in such a place
words get in the way.

September 2017

TRADITIONS

four old friends around the campfire
beneath a magic harvest moon
tiny red mars riding shotgun
glowing embers bring out the best
stories of the past year unfold
laughter erupts over days gone by
they were single when this began
now each one has a family
wives children grandkids to love
another year has passed by
leaves just beginning to turn
venus and saturn shine down
despite the cold tent and hard ground
some traditions are priceless
throw another log on the fire

October 2020

OUTSIDE LIFE

September calls me outside
give up your indoor life
follow me into the wood
the leaves are still green
days are warm and dry
walk the soft forest paths
silent steps look listen
like an Indian scout
knowing every inch of land
each ripple in the stream
where the bullfrog leaps
the turtle suns on a log
the eagle has its nest
deer lie in the tall grass
cool nights bring a deep sleep

soon the trees will catch fire
ablaze in orange and red
nights will glow with embers
to ward off the damp chill
and hypnotize the soul
when October does flee
living the outside life
will mean leaving this place
walking the southern trail
where pine trees are plenty
the nights are not so long
just long enough for dreams
of Spring warmth and new life
outside life never stops
though time stands still inside

September 2019

Silence

We stare into the campfire
speaking to us in flames
snaps pops and cracks
listening intently
warmth fills our being
the silent magic palpable
touching us like smoke
blown into our faces
by the shifting wind

three old friends gathered
beneath the hunter's moon
pondering past campfires
when more friends sat
under October's spell
before the cold silence
invites the tall trees
that quietly oversee us
to undress for winter

daddy longlegs scrambles
silently into the shadows
away from the glowing fire
seeking shelter underneath
bent and browning ferns
the big dipper gently
simmers in the dark sky
its silent gift of light
a timeless journey.

October 2016

Décor

Three pheasants race by under the November sky
exotic colors glisten on flapping feathers
just above the silent field of dry brown goldenrod
each stalk crowned with a delicate cream tiara
a mobile in this still life awaiting a vase

geese fly south as the super moon fades in sky blue
gunshots break the reverie as hunters prepare
sighting in their rifles for the first day of buck
muddy deer trail slices down the steep embankment
no bucks to be seen as the four-wheeler buzzes past

three crows fight for purchase against the cold north wind
trees shake and whisper about the coming first snow
brown oak leaves gently to and fro before landing
pungent aroma evokes long lost forest walks
two blue jays alight playing tag in creaking firs

wild grape vines--nearly fruitless--drape over bare trees
a new carpet rests beneath the undressed forest
bright design of yellow maple and trailing pine
gray tree bark with lichen medallions stiffen
all resolve will be soon tested by the deep frosts

nature redecorates with each fleeting season
would that its quiet beauty never fail to stir

November 2016

Just Passing Through

the cold wind is blowing again
we should be leaving tomorrow
but instead we're staying put
too sick for the thousand mile drive
south on interstate ninety-five
through the old confederacy
that seems to have risen again
rearing its political head
resisting the march of progress
instead promising to bring back
a place that left many behind
tradition never goes gently

memories of other campaigns
names on signs speak of battlefields
bucktail brigade so far from home
marching south after gettysburg
wilderness cold harbor five forks
chasing lee toward surrender
cotton fields a curiosity
for this native son of the north
who came of age on southern rock
skynard allman marshall tucker
shoveling PA snow not coal
before searching out a new place

the civil war now upon us
sheds not blood but sows division
tearing apart friend and sibling
a truce will not mend this divide
north south east west all are fair game

no airwave is safe from the news
take care in your choice of topic
even the weather is suspect

I am just passing through these lands
on the way to Florida sun
hoping to leave winter behind
looking for that fountain of youth
trying to stay ahead of time
a smile goes a long way anywhere

February 2020

Heartbeats

lone gull gracefully flaps
over the rippled sea
green beneath pure sky blue
sunrise soon will be here
waves caress the shoreline
gulf's heartbeat is steady
twenty times a minute
one-third as fast as mine
both of us living bodies
full of deep mystery
watch and listen closely
learning by osmosis

January 22, 2021

To Touch

windless before sunrise
vast expanse glasslike
pelican glides inches
above the pink mirror
coming sun reflects
four flocks whirl
unfettered
unlike me

seashells
draw my eye down
exoskeleton sculptures
atop moist white sand
once life lived within
now something to touch
rub between soft fingers
seashells seem eternal
not so human skin
we wither within
leave a memory
nothing to touch

March 2021

Sunset

dreamlike fog envelopes the shore
wavesound assures the sea is near
water the shade of antique glass
white foam disappears into sand
pelican glides under the mist
empty beach bespeaks silence
don't mourn the orange setting sun
daytime dreams so rarely surface
best to breathe them up inside
refill your being with magic
maybe then they will reappear
when you are most in need

January 23, 2021

Beyond Time

morning tea at the beach
just me and the gulls
gentle waves brush the sand
gaze west over the gulf
sun rising to the east
soft breezes from the south
up north my home shivers
pen records the moment

magic is all about
night and day almost equal
brown pelican lands offshore
since time immemorial
nature needs no volume
earth has its own soundtrack
one that is beyond time
to listen is to live

January 2021

Shoveling Snow

Sometimes it's light and airy
other times wet and heavy
it will blow around to fill up
the space you just emptied
hands and feet get cold and wet
snow goes down your neck
and the lifting hurts my back
be careful shoveling out cars
shovels, like kids, like to hit things
shoveling snow is a good time
to see seldom seen neighbors
who have been hibernating
especially if they need help shoveling
the snowplow always goes by
late at night whenever
i'm finished my digging out the driveway
just so I don't feel too good about
all the white stuff I've already moved
before it re-filled the driveway
sometimes it rains and freezes
after the snow has fallen
making it much harder
to shovel or to even stay upright
the plastic shovel is wider but worthless
with ice while the metal shovel
only holds a little of the fluffy white
you can chip away each hour
or wait until the sky stops falling
depending on your temperament
and philosophy of shoveling

soon enough the snow turn from white
to gray and brown and even yellow
and the piles beside the sidewalk
melt slowly into mud from the rain
maybe this time we can put the shovel
back in the garage until next winter.

2015

Missing the Snow

Wander down white sandy beach
in place of shoveling the blizzard
white sea-foam washing ashore
watching snow fall through glass
collect sea shells for grandchildren
waiting days for the snowplow
bike along cool blue gulf shoreline
hoping the electric does not depart
gaze on snow white egret still-fully hunting
don snowshoes for neighborhood adventure
converse with white-haired "snowbirds"
cross country ski on unplowed streets

happy hour sunsets with northern refugees
making snow angels with the grandkids
stay within the white lines on I-95
shoveling out elder neighbors
beguiled by elegant Sandhill Cranes
anxious to wash salt-splattered car
pull on raincoat in the warm squall
boots, parka, gloves hat live by the door
sweep fine beach sand from my shoes
digging a snow tunnel to sidewalk
wishing we could stay longer in Florida
grandkids beckon us home to snowy cold

February 2016

Pining

left the cool empty north covered in firs
landed back home to heat humidity traffic
black-eyed susans a lone ray of sunshine
brightening a backyard full of brown grass
cicada chatter and cricket song abound
this familiar place now feels foreign
the skyline had changed during my absence

neighbors had cut down the big pine tree
that made looking out the back windows
seem like gazing upon somewhere other
than this aging streetcar suburb
it wore furrowed plates of reddish bark
while flexing a strong cactus-like limb
many decades old it predated every neighbor

the big conifer colored the skyline green
its pine needles filled the gutters and yard
the sharp hard pinecones a favorite of mine
so too with the gray squirrels and grandkids
unruffled by the wind snow sleet and rain
the robust pine was cut down in its prime
wish I knew its family--pitch, pond or loblolly

the gray six-foot stump stares back at me
over the backyard fence as a dying reminder
wood shavings lie on the ground waiting
to become one with the dense clay soil
the northern skyline is filled with wires
and a yellow house too big for its lot
life goes on for the tiny brown ants

September 2016

An Extra Blanket in April

The second week of April two weeks after Easter
not far off groundhog assured us of an early Spring
I follow the old road west walking downstream
snow blows and spits as Piney Creek sets the pace
patiently awaiting waders when trout come in season

snow-covered hemlocks nod like ballet dancers on tiptoe
branches and trunk aligned in perfect symmetry
dozen robins hop along the road ahead of me
looking for a snow-free place to converse
not the Spring meander they had in mind either

slush in the roadside ditch looks like frogs' eggs
snow coats the leafless branches of an immature tree
like white velvet on the horns of a young buck
narrow deer trail slices down the steep bank
empty field where travel trailers once laughed
rode the school bus with the kids who lived here

walk quietly past the many chain-link cages of dogs
before one sounds the alarm and a chorus of howls erupts
seems like the owners like this cacophony
listening to the barks from the inside peeking out
who or what lies hidden in the small white house

around the bend yellow "Posted" signs proliferate
no trespassing it warns on plastic nailed into trees
two whitetails scamper across the road without even
a glance at the warnings not to enter this private land
freedom to move about this land a part of their being
stride past the old homestead I once dreamed of buying
forty-five minutes of walking without meeting a car

lots of yellow metal poles marking underground gas lines
natural gas pumping station generator breaks the silence
where is the family I knew who lived on this spot
"In God we Trust" sign stands alongside a mailbox
reminder of Easter or the looming election

march past where the old coal tipple used to sit
before some angry miners burned it down one night
railroad ties spikes and rails have all gone away
flattening our pennies on the rails a thing of the past
dreams of riding the caboose as far as it would take us
now fond figments of a swiftly aging imagination

walking amidst my past at three miles an hour
memories falling to earth like the April snowflakes
once knew who lived in every solitary house
now I'm the stranger on these silent back roads
listening to my own spirit whisper welcome home

April 2016

BUFFALO BULL SITS DOWN

Sitting upon an Appaloosa
under an ancient pine
pondering if this was to be
the end of their great line
would the Great Spirit grace him
with one more victory
could this be the place
where he would become history
these Black Hills had always
been sacred to his Lakota tribe
now they were on the run
like prey, with nowhere to hide
beside the bullsnake, badger, bobcat,
 prairie dog, pronghorn and porcupine
among the hoodoos and buttes, canyons,
gullies, shortgrass, ponderosa pine.

Might the Great Spirit transform them
into bison until there was no more fear
Lakota had shared the land
with these majestic nomads for over 11000 years
the bison that kept them warm and fed
would soon be sharing the Lakota tears
his people only killed to live, while the white mans' guns
killed for no reason
living with the land, generation after generation,
all things have a season
from the sacrifice of the Sun Dance
to prophet's powerful Ghost Dance
Sitting Bull, the holy man,
invoked the Great Spirit for almighty guidance.

In 1876, when Custer came in search
of the Lakota at the Little Big Horn
they wanted only to be left alone
in their Black Hills to hunt and be born
Sitting Bull did not fight at the Little Big Horn
but only spoke the Spirit's words
the railroad further scarred their Black Hills
and brought the ever-growing herds
treaty or not, gold and settlers in the Black Hills
meant the Lakota must be gone
wanted by the United States Army, Sitting Bull fled
with a band to Saskatchewan
The holy man returned in 1881
to surrender and give up his gun
Sitting Bull asked his captors,
who would teach his young son?

Forty police officers surrounded
the Lakota chief's house before dawn
arresting the holy man on December 15, 1890
afraid he would be gone
fearing Sitting Bull would flee to join
those who practiced the Ghost Dance
the sacred dance that joined the spirits
of living and dead, urging nonviolence
foretold that the native dead would return
to a joyful life without the white man
gunned down, unarmed, the spirit of Tatanka Iyotake
returned to Mother Earth
from the sacrificial Sun Dance
to prophetic Ghost Dance, a proud legacy
Sitting Bull, the Lakota holy man,
became one with the Great Mystery.

March 2015

Thoreau's Favorite

white pines always remind me of home
old friends who say so much with silence
strong limbs stretch the wooded horizon
delicate branches float to the sky
towers of grace amid summer's leaves
breath of pine scent in July's closeness
awning of shade under August sun
perfect green patch in autumn's best quilt
beacons of green in winter's dull gray
brown needles refresh the woodland rug
sticky white pitch catches my fingers
straight gray spine reaches ever skyward

stands tall behind the family home
holds the dishes in mom's cabinet
watches over us as the years pass
whisper softly to your hemlock kin
share your pine cones on the forest floor
you give refuge to squirrels and birds
when big winds blow you creak a warning
your long planks have built many old barns
breaks my heart when you split in a storm
must agree there is no finer tree
have a big favor of you to ask
would you be my box when I have passed

August 2019

A Dying Art

it all begins in summertime
a trip picture of just us two
nature is often the backdrop
mountains lakes rivers waterfalls
no one there to take the photo
sometimes the tiny tripod works

a theme does not come easily
but Evie always teases one out
for the letter that tags along
a year painted on a single page
to many friends we never see
adventures milestones family

thumb through the tattered address list
some folks are no longer with us
others are now beyond our reach
add a personal note to each
how much is postage to Finland
hope they all get there by Christmas

January 2020

American Hero

someday she might be the most famous one
buried here in the Fort Hill Cemetery
a hilly maze of trees   lawn   stone
where once stood a Cayuga castle

this morning we are alone among the dead
the gravity of history weighs heavy upon us
in this silent place on a July morning under
an ashen sky that has just stopped sobbing
her headstone reads

Harriet Tubman Davis
heroine of the underground railroad
Nurse and Scout in the Civil War
Born about 1820 in Maryland
Died March 10, 1913 in Auburn, NY
"Servant of God, Well done"

memories of a grade five field trip
lonely stone Pennsylvania farmhouse
surrounded by bare fields and hills
halfway between Maryland and Ontario
move in single file to the dirt cellar
gape wide-eyed at dusty secret passages
once a stop on the underground railroad

it was something magical unexplainable
to a young boy from an all-white area
how could a railroad go underground
all the way from down South to Canada
fifty years later the magic reappears

Harriet Tubman is my Rosetta Stone
her story isn't magic realism it's real

awestruck after visiting her property
purchased from friend William Seward
now a museum to this American hero
thirteen missions saved seventy people
a conductor who never lost a passenger
led an armed assault in the civil war
humanitarian   suffragist   patriot
five feet tall she always gave it her all
sure hope she makes it onto the Twenty

November 2017

SUOMI WHISPERS

Old boreal forest silently invites
walk amidst my green and rock
long hidden under ages of ice
breathe in pine there is no clock

reach down to pick ripe berries
sit upon shore's pink granite
gaze at passing baltic ferries
long days like another planet

ladle cool water over fiery rocks
sweat drips under clouds of steam
splash into lakes from wooden docks
sauna ritual a recurring dream

ponder the long nights soon to possess
winter approaches in her clean white dress

November 2016
("Suomi" is Finland in Finnish)

ERRATICS

we sit atop the giant boulder
abandoned on this coniferous
hillside during the last ice age
like Iroquois braves resting
after a long trek up and down
the steep hills bathed in shadow
by the ancient hemlock kings
who hide these huge gray rocks
adorned in lichen and moss
from the prying eyes of the sun

far below our forest castle
the stream dances easily
over algae-covered rocks
beside us small hemlocks
sprout from crevices
nourished by centuries
silent decaying matter
somehow finding
this sacred place

May 2016

TREVERIEN

Treverien takes me in
an American refugee
seeking stone and pastry
fleeing the land of the free
where everything is for sale
this is where I will begin
hidden away in Brittany
have become a long lost son

Treverien embraces me
tall poplars blow in the wind
hug the shores of the green Rance
muse on the sandy towpath
thin river boats go slowly
tall stone steeples draw me up
small bridges invite me over
days that never seem to end

Treverien swallows me
baguettes and brie all around
bonjour is always at hand
blackberries begging a bite
two centuries is not old here
windows and doors stay open
two feet or two wheels are best
slowing down brings meaning close

Treverien exhales me
shows another side of life
at home so far from my home
language does not silence me
ancient DNA wakes up
place is where we all begin
dreams are the heartbeat of life
we may never meet again

September 2018

CYCLING

Life expands when you are pedaling. Cycling has been a big part of my life since my first solo bike tour of Nova Scotia in 1984—a magical experience. I met my wife while cycling the Oregon and California coasts and almost all of our summer vacations are experienced on our tandem bicycle.

Lost Again

somewhere in French countryside
astride a tandem bicycle
packed with all our belongings
no cell phone or GPS
knowing only a few French words
what kind of vacation is this

a new destination each day
chosen only last evening
pouring over pages of maps
towns with names we cannot pronounce
sometimes we follow a river
like explorers in days of old

a childlike sense of adventure
long daylight gives you lots of time
this world invites discovery
the goodness of strangers warms us
coming through when you need them most
people have so much in common

a friend just waiting to be met
language overflows from the heart
a smile is never mispronounced
getting lost is finding yourself
somewhere deep inside a moment
being lost gets under your skin

September 2108

Bellona Avenue Descent

Flying downhill
As fast as a car
Avoiding potholes
Wind in your face
Feeling kidlike
A bird in flight
Leaves floating down
Wishing it was longer
Slowing as the hill flattens
Pedaling as the road rises
Praying there is room for both cars and me
Smooth road gives way to bumpy blacktop
Shifting into an easier gear under labored breath
Bicycling and living are both a series of ups and downs

2014

Red Epaulettes

pedaling around Druid Lake
Red-winged blackbird calls
o-ka-leee o-ka-leee look at me
standing atop a tall stone post
red epaulettes trimmed in white
add credence to the shrill call
next loop around he calls
o-ka-leee before flying off
back to his post
in the cattails
at the water's edge
calling o-ka-leee
to the floating ducks

May 2016

Montebello

on this third ride with her new knee
we keep the lake close beside us
circling around like clock hands
clockwise at fifteen mph
at one end gulls soar squawk land bob
new knee loosening with each lap
one point three miles just long enough
so the laps don't go too quickly
tandem bike responding so well
since our last ride in September

mid-day monday rides are a treat
retirement has some nice perks
walkers have a lane beside us
wave to little ones in strollers
resist jumping on the pace line
of three single bikes that pass by
helmets down legs spin small circles
front rider breaking the west wind
would have jumped on with the old knee
pushing hard to keep up their pace

new knee must be brought on slowly
perhaps we could wear a big sign
spelling out new knee in training
a lifetime of competition
is not so easily tamped down
the other three knees are gentle
with their mechanical sibling
you must work as hard as you can
montebello is nice and flat
provence's mountains lie in wait

twenty-six miles is enough
march's soft breath cool upon our cheeks
the tandem's wheels come to a stop
when you are working together
even flat mountains have beauty

March 2020

HEROES

Cycling through Gettysburg
on a gray Spring day
wild mustard yellows
amidst white dandelion
gone to seed like a clown's head
red-winged blackbirds to and fro
from stone marker to split rail fence
newly emerged honeysuckle
drapes herself over a green bush
not time yet for her perfume
all that lives is now growing

from high atop his marble post
Custer looks down upon
cornstalks mown down
along East Cavalry Field
in this place
his Michigan brigade
repulsed Stuart's charges
winning the day

further into the battlefield
children climb upon
the rocks of Devil's Den
we get a smile and thumbs up
as we pump the tandem
over the steep rise
look across to Little Round Top
where Chamberlain held his ground
around the bend
an Irish Wolfhound lies
beneath a Celtic cross

on Confederate Avenue
Lee sits astride Traveler
studying the Union lines
nearby lies the farm
where Eisenhower watched
over this sacred ground

being here
leads me to reflect
even heroes die.

May 2017

March Ride

we stop and take off layers
not sure what to wear today
first warm day of the year
muddy tractor rumbles past
manure spreader close behind
swerve to miss brown droppings
pungent scent wafts from the field
soon life will sprout from beneath
tires gravel-voiced on winter grit

first ride in the countryside
stiff breeze over brown fields
memories of paper kites
launched in march at grandma's farm
spiraling down to earth
another run for lift off
paper and wood crash down
maybe the tail wasn't right
freedom is so fleeting

memories of rides long past
young kid on a red huffy
country road under wide tires
after winter's long cold
exploring paths new and old
scent of today's wind hopeful
cows watch as we crest the hill
promises of rides to come
winds of change are all we know

March 2021

APRILIS

tulips and daffodils smile at us
as we pedal by on this April day
Spring climbed up our front steps
begging us to come out to play
glide past grand homes on Roland Ave
come to a stop over the Jones Falls
where once the mills made cotton duck
a photographer means the time is right
the famous visitors must be at home
two pairs of Yellow-crowned Night Herons
building their nests high over the stream
on the long gray arm of a sycamore tree
a regal bird worthy of its great name
they flew here from Florida to breed
seeing them for the first time is magic

we pedal past tennis courts empty pool
an old cemetery and cherry blossoms
some of Druid Lake is being remade
underground water tanks will take years
no more loops around this urban gem
big machines build nice new homes
for the zoo's elephants and giraffes
we huff and puff up Mountain Pass
as a zoo train filled with families
approaches the charming chimpanzees
how can a Wednesday be more fun
lunch is calling so we pedal on
through the back of Johns Hopkins U
students making their way to class
Spring brings out the best in us

Sherwood Gardens in stately Guilford
the site of our brief picnic lunch
a lovely park famous for flowers
tulips, daffodils, and azaleas regale us
from our stone bench the colors dazzle
we refuel with sliced apple and PB&J
back atop the bicycle built for two
one more lap around this sumptuous park
soaking in the splendor with like minds
ride through two more colleges en route
Loyola and Notre Dame of Maryland
wishing for some knowledge osmosis
to offset the forgetfulness of age
smile upon cozy ponds on Spring Lake Way
so much to savor--on this April day

April 2019

THE ROUTE MATTERS

july ride on north central rail trail
lincoln's final passage was on this route
going home to illinois from DC
lincoln rode this way to gettysburg too
there he delivered his famous address
black lives matter signs grace our neighborhood
emancipation proclamation
still striving to be realized today
as john lewis pauses in the rotunda
before his final ride for freedom
on the way to his heavenly home
his lifelong quest for justice our gift

today this rails to trail is well used
filled with nature and quiet movement
bike riders runners walkers some with masks
unaware of its place in history
sojourn with nature and covid escape
snap dragons bide their time to flower
shaded ferns waft the freshest of scents
few small raspberries left on jagged vines
tree canopy for most of the route
the gunpowder though low beckons floaters
restrooms are closed at monkton station
covid means portable toilets only

trail climbs slightly as I pedal north
toward PA line and new freedom
all sorts of people are out today
each one is equal on the trail of life
ring my bell as I pass on the left
trail etiquette is in short supply
sorry it's hard to stay six feet apart

miss the old days when the trail was empty
still love this path and its history
so many ways to travel through time
the route of life can never be plotted
till our journey is finally written

July 2020

Under the Covid Sky

not much bests a tandem ride
in summer's lush countryside
far away from news inside
most of it sad these days
death, lost jobs, social unrest
these back roads bring us freedom
our view is one with nature
pedals spin their smooth cadence
warm air caresses our faces
we are bound for littlestown

it's easy to feel small now
under covid's watchful gaze
hawk's underside shines on high
sky is plane-less baby blue
cirrus and cumulus clouds
float gently beneath heaven
wheat field stubble glows golden
grass browns under summer sun
milkweed awaits the monarch
while we await the vaccine

weeds flaunt their green abundance
while hope is in short supply
roadside dressed with queen anne's lace
black-eyed susans dot the land
bike tires grasp the warm pavement
chain clatters to the next gear
slow down for new tar and chip
we wear masks in the sub shop
sit out on the curb to eat
savor shade cold drink rest

moments of peace are hard fought
after all we have been through
surgery's wrath covid's reign
riding together through life
pumping up hills coasting down
forty miles is just enough
time to remember life's joy
trying hard not to cave in
beneath uncertainty's weight
under the vast covid sky

July 2020

Among the Amish

Late September in Lancaster County
after a big whiff of drying tobacco
in a yellow barn with open sides
we overtake an Amish horse and buggy
on a bicycle built for two
one horsepower against four aging legs
it seemed like a good time
until the road rose
we push hard on the pedals
clip clop clip clop clip clop
the Amish nod and say hello
guess we are still the "English"
we cycle past the tidy farms
homemade sign reminds us to repent
no Halloween decorations here
fields of orange pumpkins
yellow shocks of dried corn
dappled cows mirror the clouds
draft horses pull hay wagons
look twice at an older Amish woman
who resembles a great aunt
barefoot girl mowing the lawn
marigolds shine beside a waning garden
children playing ball at recess
near their one-room schoolhouse
we coast through a covered bridge
a bird house with a back door
boards thumping under bike tires
swerve to avoid horse manure
nice to be on the road with the Amish
moving only as fast as the legs will spin
no texting loud music or road rage
from the handsome black buggies

makes me want to become Amish
living a physical life on the land
going only as fast as the buggy
resisting the snares of technology
that entwine us like bales of hay
beings unwilling to break the bonds
to escape under our own steam.

October 2015

Crossing the Road

Grasshoppers sunbathe on blacktop
drawn by the warm black ribbon
albino woolly bear crawls quickly
making me feel better about winter
a few more pedal strokes and coast
turn to miss all rust-colored kin
ride further and spy its cousin
small black stripes at tip and tail
separated by a fuzzy brown band

with no consensus on color
how am I to predict the winter
woolly bears emerge in the fall
change from eggs to caterpillar
survive the cold by freezing solid
thaw out in spring and shed the fur
coming out as isabella tiger moth
so many changes in one year
bike tires murmur on blacktop

monarch floats by in air ballet
has it missed its flight to Mexico
shoo a cricket off the blacktop
while stopped to remove a jacket
swerve to miss the black walnuts
waiting for squirrels to bury them
green caterpillar crosses the road
looking for long gone tomatoes
the october road calls to those
who jump crawl fly or pedal.

October 2016

Lost

Slight turn of the handlebars
steers the tandem bike around
a fresh mound of horse manure
left by a shiny black horse
pulling the handsome buggy
an Amish family within
patiently going from here
to there sharing the road
they return our wave and smiles
on this sunny October Thursday
no place we would rather be

another turn of the handlebars
steers the tandem bike around
an orange and black woolly bear
hurriedly crossing the road
as a fellow traveler
also in orange and black
a Monarch butterfly
making its way to Mexico
floats past our helmeted heads
wish we could tag along
Indian summer won't last

around the bend a team of horses
pulls an antique corn picker
through tall sand-colored stalks
grabbing the hard yellow ears
leaving the rest to be baled up
into bedding for livestock

each road name paints a story
of the Pennsylvania Dutch landscape
paradise lane little beaver sawmill
stumptown cider mill conestoga creek
amishtown musser school farmersville

it's easy to get lost here
harvest sunshine warms all
before long we realize it
we are off the cue sheet
our next turn was back there
we are used to getting lost
it is part of riding a bike
losing yourself to discover
what is around the next bend
sometimes making a new friend

we stop to check our paper map
and spy a teenage Amish girl
deep in the window's well
only her head above ground
cleaning out the autumn leaves
before winter's cold blanket
we call over and she comes out
followed by two white Labs
and a curious little sister
in her long dress and bonnet

she patiently listens big eyes
making contact all the while
her sincere accent captivates
no smart phone GPS among us
she locates us on the map
and points back the way we came
the road will be on your right
past the one-room schoolhouse
before we mount and ride off
on the bicycle built for two
she smiles and says if you get lost
you can always come back and ask

November 2017

Earthbound

bike tires crunch curled dry leaves
like quick taps on a snare drum
yellow-brown leaves flutter down
joining siblings on the ground
gray skies match the country's mood
week before election day
hawk's peal breaks the near silence
welcome sound in vulture filled sky
dry oak leaf perfume permeates
bygone days within awaken

general custer stands tall
atop his pedestal
here on east cavalry field
surveys the autumn landscape
silent cannons face east
twas here on the third day
stuart's cavalry was stopped
say a silent prayer
for those who never got up
resting here forever

gettysburg yard sign says
"this battle was fought
because black lives matter"
mourning dove launches low
startled by our approach
swerve to miss brown snake's slithers
zigzagging across warm pavement
winter wheat sprouts green
from this year's corn field
all things belong to the earth

November 2020

Oasis

we ride a circuitous line
on the bicycle built for two
come heat cold wind sunshine
our go-to ride zigs to the zoo

for years we never rode south
past the nearby city line
when pedaling from the house
missing out on sights sublime

the park never fails to inspire
much like a Wyeth landscape
William Wallace easy to admire
standing tall beside the lake

say hello to our nameless friends
while looping through Druid Hill
yellow leaves crunch as we ascend
spying a giraffe is a thrill

coast past tennis courts pool
basketball softball playgrounds
frisbee golf sure looks cool
walkers leashed to wagging hounds

gentlemen shining cars under trees
we up our cadence as drummers keep time
smiling runners invoke a cool breeze
mountain pass is our favorite big climb

ancient oaks bestowed the park's name
only Fairmount and Central came before
a modest beauty she seeks no fame
urban nature has so much in store

a sanctuary for all seasons
framed by the downtown skyline
cycling here is well beyond reason
since 1860 an oasis sublime

such a lovely place to hide
cannot wait for our next ride

November 2017

Harvest

the park in western Maryland is empty
we set out on this gray October Friday
pedaling hard into the stiff cold wind
jackets, warm gloves, hats, layers, tights, booties
only yesterday it was eighty-one

this bike ride is a yearly ritual
age does not make it any easier
swerve to miss the litter of black walnuts
with plaintive eyes beneath spotted bodies
the silent Holsteins seem to ask us why

we pass many who were recently silenced
rabbit, squirrel, deer, raccoon, snake, woollies
two soaring vultures circle high above
like hands on a fast moving airborne clock
these undertakers have much work to do

white stone farmhouses make us want to come in
arched stone bridges help us cross swollen streams
mud and small ponds cover many brown fields
leaves seem to fall before turning color
winter wheat is a welcome sign of life

uphills are your friend on cold days like this
pushing helps to warm frozen fingers, toes
lots of sniffling from my cold runny nose
cornfields in stubble, brown soybeans still wait
we forge on dreaming of a warm shower

Sharpsburg warms our spirits with a rest stop
lunch is al fresco sitting on a curb
fresh Amish apple dumplings make me smile
days such as this make us laugh at ourselves
forty-nine miles is a long ride today

cycling through Antietam never gets old
site of the bloodiest American day
it gave Lincoln hope to Emancipate
white Dunker church is a beacon of hope
we pedal home thankful to be alive

November 2018

The Death Still Haunts Him

the death still haunts him
a fellow cyclist hit from behind
riding in a marked bicycle lane
on a sunny Saturday afternoon
the first one after Christmas
melancholy Irish tunes and songs
momentarily soothed the pain
and lifted the worry about
his own defenselessness
while pedaling on car-filled streets
sad songs of fleeing the famine
fighting in the American Civil War
riding with Custer at the Little Big Horn
living with the deadly and divisive Troubles
allowed his spirit to commiserate
with those aboard the coffin ships
and forever lying in unmarked graves
the fiddle, whistle, pipes, and flute
need no words as they rise and fall
like his own feelings in the mournful air
may the fallen cyclist rest in peace.

January 2015

Requiem for a Possum

Slight turn of the handlebar
steers the skinny bike tires
around the still gray mound
just south of Gettysburg
lifeless grin over blacktop
must have wandered on the road
during a moonlight forage

hope it wasn't carrying young
inside its marsupial pouch
this South American immigrant
named by the Algonquin tribe
nocturnal nomadic solitary
whisper a prayer for its spirit
as I pedal 'round the bend

should I turn around and stop
drag the corpse off the road
act as a pall bearer of sorts
before the vultures and crows
swoop down to handle
the final arrangements
according to nature's laws

no way to notify next of kin
I mourn with leafless trees
wind sighs a timeless hymn
cold tears will rain down soon
from the somber gray sky
hope my prayers for the departed
are finished for this ride.

February 2017

January Pedaling

hope my fingers warm up
before my toes get cold
early january sunshine
does not give off much heat
pedal into cold west wind
no incentive to go fast
ring bell and call "on your left"
slow down and go around
walkers on the narrow path
swerve to avoid broken glass
tossed from last night's car
hope I don't get a flat tire
too cold to stop and fix it
fingers need warmth for repairs
greet a passing cyclist
covered up from toe to head
red-tailed hawk glides above
blue jays land in a bare tree
pileated woodpecker
looking so much like Woody
taps into a smooth gray trunk
silent geese float like decoys
avoiding the winter wind
every bike ride
is a good one

September 2019

For the Birds

the Great Egret stares intently
a brilliant white-winged flower
shin deep in tea-colored water
next to knobbed Bald Cypress knees
beside the gray asphalt bike trail
Ontarians on bikes swoosh past
admiring the statuesque fowl

big smiles as the line pedals by
happy to be flying along
here on the Withlacoochee trail
temperatures in the seventies
joining others from the far north
basking beneath Florida sun
back home the polar vortex freezes

like-minded birds of a feather
flocking in RV caravans
playing instead of shoveling
breathing in ibis and egret
pushing away migration thoughts
on this divine January day
some snowbirds never see the snow

February 2019

TRAIL FRIENDS

it is our last ride of the year
on our favored florida trail
start down the ribbon of blacktop
three river otters disappear
life's nymphs are often so fleeting
great egrets stalk in perfect white
gopher tortoises remind us
we are the new kids around here
palmettos wave in the warm breeze
mother gator basks with three young
beside the tannic cypress swamp
anhinga dries its arching wings
standing upon a submerged tree
wood stork studies the shallow pools
black snake slides west we pedal south
cattle eye us through barbed wire fence
worry for the sleek green turtle
calmly floating where gators live
hawk silently watches us coast
brown lizards vanish in a flash
live oaks play host to spanish moss
savor this flat ride through nature
never tire of this new flora
spring peepers squeak as we finish
tandem stowed for the long drive home
it is hard to leave such a place
new friends to be found every mile

April 2021

GRANDCHILDREN

"Let's play" is music to my ears. The grandkids have breathed new life into me. Seeing the world through their eyes is a priceless process of discovery. We learn from each other's smiles. If only I had their energy.

Weightless

after weeks of coaxing
the grandchildren win
talk me into getting on
the big blue trampoline
in their back yard
next to the swing set
on this warm autumn eve
the coming dark
brings us close

hoping not to break it
I sit in the middle
throwing squishy balls
at their shins and feet
trying to trip them up
as they circle round me
they run fall bounce
loving this new game
Colin Zach Zoe and me

we look up to a crescent moon
a planet glows beside it
might be Mars or Venus I say
what planet are we on
four year old Colin asks
we are on planet Earth
the older two reply
mommy calls from inside
it's time for dessert

September 2019

Breaking Bread at Springlake

They tear pieces from the yellow slices
stuffing it into their hungry mouths
eagerly swallowing the soft bread
like the fish and ducks who live here
in these four small shaded pools
on this warm October afternoon
sun slanting through big cedars
a glorious reason for our excursion
most likely the last of the season

soon the water is filled with bread
the large koi slowing rising to look
before inhaling the soggy slice
our three ducklings are two four six
hungry for bread and adventure
show them how to roll each piece
into a small ball that flies further
before sinking quickly in still water
devoured by a school of small fish

the older two splash in a stone chute
a watery path not meant for feet
soon clothes are dripping with smiles
the mallards are happy to eat
fighting over the 99 cent loaf
the competition is contagious
Zach aims for the boy ducks
Zoe throws toward the girl ducks
Colin smiles when his bread hits water
the fish eat what the ducks miss

bread almost done by pond three
feeders getting full fatigue follows

lone yellow flower floats on lily pads
find a duck feather at the final pond
hand it to Zach for close inspection
Zoe climbs across the stone waterfall
bread now gone Colin in my arms
Zach calmly walks into the flock
delicately holding the small feather
"do you want your feather back?"

October 2016

An Exotic Gem

would you like to go to the zoo
yes, yes said zach jumping for joy
big sister was in kindergarten
baby brother was taking a nap
when are we going to get there
why do we have to park so far away
will you carry me pop pop
rare request from this tenacious tot

what should we see first
I asked looking at the "treasure map"
polar bears he shouted with joy
our search for polar bears came up empty
the sky a cloudless blue over their pen
sign said the polar bears were staying
inside on this warm October day

around the bend things looked up
a leopard stalked close to the fence
next door lived two cheetahs
zach's favorite--he loves all things fast
looking right a huge gray rhino kicked up dust
sharing its big field with gazelle, zebra and ostrich
zach climbed on all the rocks—real and man-made
we discovered along our yellow-brick road

the three small elephants looked a bit forlorn
we gazed down upon them from above
grabbing chunks of straw with their trunks
elephants are vegetarian I told zach
I'm a vegetarian and I eat meat he said
he would turn four in five weeks
sharing a moment of fall never to be repeated

the path led us past prairie dog, pink flamingo
porcupine, rattle snake, fox, giraffe, and tortoise
lemurs jumped around like spiderman
zach wishing he could be inside with them
penguins hold us captive waddling in black and white
playfully diving in and transforming into fish
reminded of my first trip to the zoo in fifth grade
a day that sparkles in memory like an exotic gem

our allotted two and a half hours now gone
we stopped once more to watch the penguins
just one more minute he said each time I started to move
the prairie dogs stood still as Zach yelled a final goodbye
once through the front gate he jumped into my arms
back at the car and buckled in
my fellow adventurer was soon fast asleep

October 2016

First Things

it feels good to be in first grade
magical things seems to happen
a sparkling october grandparents day
zach waves a shy smile as I come in
before coming over to hug me
I sit down on the blue folding chair

zach takes me back to his wooden desk
I sharpen three dull yellow pencils
from his leather pencil case
before we start the day's lesson
two boys together playmates
rhyming words filling the page

zach faces away standing tall and still
I trace his silhouette on black paper
try not to tremble with joy
do the same for classmate eleanor
her chestnut curls and glasses glow
she has no grandparent to help

later zach sits on my lap
my arms around his small waist
I select from scattered slips
traits describing my dear boy
loyal strong active curious thoughtful
zach is too much for words

zach and I share a special bond
seven fun years in the making
infant toddler first grader
sad to see this class visit end
parting is hard when you are seven
when is our next play-date

November 2019

Learning and Teaching

Like many good things it happens only once a year
we smiling grandparents are overjoyed to be here
the primary school cafeteria is our waiting room
this is generations day our big chance to swoon
a photo with your grandchild is just such a boon

Zoe is all smiles in a sleeveless summer dress
first grade class begins with a morning meeting
how are you feeling today Mrs. C calls on three
Zoe's hand shoots up and she joyfully shares
I'm feeling happy because my Pop Pop is here

our lesson today is on the many joys of autumn
I admire the teacher's energy—control—routine
Zoe grabs her school laptop and quickly logs in
love being here beside her in the small chair
classroom walls shine with laminated wisdom

reminds me of student teaching decades ago
grade two in Oregon the little kids just glowed
should have switched majors to elementary ed
so many classrooms over the years—most were fun
starting long ago with Mrs. Mills in grade one

at home we play school with Zoe as the teacher
many more smiles than frowns she's no preacher
Zach plays the good student and I play the bad
Zoe's so good that playing bad makes me sad
if she follows in my footsteps I'd be glad

soon my hour is over we have to trade places
it's not easy to leave all these smiling faces
grandma comes in and I take little brother Colin
walking home we stop and pet neighbor dog Yukon
there is so much to learn and love along the way

November 2017

DID *YOU* KNOW?

On our way home from kindergarten
my granddaughter has a lot to say
"did *you* know," she often begins
telling me something
she wants me to know

she has taught me many things
the names of dolls and princesses
some things I once knew well
how to laugh, hide, count, sing
pretend, play, love each second

I teach her about insects, trees
animals, flowers, playing ball
her teaching all encompassing
mine seems small

being five has a lot to offer
life seen through new eyes
keeping our minds and hearts
open—not knowing at all
if we kept learning like this
who knows—our lives might be
a surprise-filled journey

always trying new things
her love of life and fun
keeps me keenly on the run
she loves being the teacher
I love being her student

maybe I can begin like her
with a twinkle and a smile
three small words, heart singing
"did *you* know?"
I could never have known
how much there was to learn
from Zoe.

October 25, 2015

CHICKADEE

chickadee dee
chickadee dee dee
we learn about Chickadees
Colin and me
Grandma makes three
he is four and full of fun
cold January morning
Woolly Bears meet once a month

Carolina Chickadee
is Maryland's Chickadee
cute little black-capped bird
white cheeks with black beak
adds grace to winter's chill
ours has blond hair and white cheeks
he cannot fly but runs fast
jumps kicks and plays all day

we build a nest at snack time
cream cheese binds the pretzels
jelly beans inside for eggs
Colin likes the bird eggs best
Pop Pop helps to eat the nest
next we build a bird feeder
pine cone lard sunflower seeds
string to hang it from a tree

bundle up for a short hike
Miss Pam leads the way
these little birds are lively
no Chickadees to be found
though mud and ice abound
the chickadees head for home
next month will be here soon
what creature will make us croon

our chickadee loves to eat
potato chips in his seat
driving home from Woolly Bears
smiling as he munches
buckled in snug and warm
before falling fast asleep
not sure who enjoys it more
Colin Grandma or me

March 2019

FAMILY TREE

First time back in a schoolhouse in over three years
after thirty-two years of teaching this is new
the joy in my being nearly brings me to tears
Zoe smiles and pulls me aside--no one is blue
adults watch the kindergarten class sing and play
cozy room glows with art, letters, numbers, class rules
teacher filled with energy on grandparents' day
never was I happier to be in a school
we press our hands small and big in the pads of ink
our blue red green palms and fingers become a tree
wash away the colors of fun in the small sink
walking down the hall hand-in-hand fills me with glee
in the photo Zoe and I smile side by side
a grandfather's love has nowhere to hide

November 2016

DRIVING WITH COLIN

once buckled into his car seat
we both smile and the fun begins
destination does not matter
Colin often asks for a song
he likes the jersey boys cd
lollipop livens up the ride

my favorite are his questions
asking about things big and small
that five year old memory astounds
his recall of things I once said
especially about those sweet treats
that lie in wait when we get home

life becomes clearer on our drives
his cute face in the rear view mirror
reach back to grab his calf or foot
tells me of his morning at school
asks me about when I was five
cannot wait to get home and play

driving to grandmapoppop's house
eating goldfish from a ziplock
sitting tall in his booster seat
wish we could do this more often
colin and I share a history
one day he may be driving me

February 2020

Behind the Garage

Not long before dinner Colin Zach and I
go behind the garage to look for worms
a ritual we repeat nearly each week
a quest that age does not diminish
nature delights at two—four—sixty

Colin grabs the small yellow trowel
from the cluttered garage shelf
heading fast past the brown bed
of Blackeyed Susans gone to seed
Zach grabs the garden fork to attack
the decaying oak stump with relish
before stabbing the nearby mushrooms

we strike it rich as we turn over
the first brick and spy new treasure
a shiny black salamander squirms
like a moving jewel in our hands
before crawling back to the ground
two worms lie under the next brick
momentarily wriggling on small hands
until they return to the damp soil

not sure who found the dead bird first
lying there so beautiful and still
where the chain-link and wood fences meet
on top of brown mulch and dying weeds
it might have been a kind of sparrow
perfectly feathered in white brown black
maybe just killed by a neighbor's cat
let out to prowl behind the garage

grandsons use their small tools to help
dig a grave for the little songbird
each gently touches the bird's feathers
with the tool's metal before we lay it
in the hole and cover it up with dirt
the birdie's grave is near our two dead cats
I tell the boys as we mark it with a stick
Zach says I have never seen animal bones
let's dig them up and Colin echoes yeah
we mustn't disturb the dead I explain
as grandma calls out dinner is ready

October 29, 2017

Pleyen

Let's play the grandkids always say
in Middle Dutch eight centuries ago
their beloved word held the same sway
to rejoice and be glad is what they show
inside or out play always means fun
early or late play is never done

stuffed animals jump sing swing slide
dinosaurs dolls dance balls blocks cars
mud puddles puzzles seek and hide
let's play means that you are okay
size gender age color all fade away
when mixed up in a good round of play

before the grandkids re-taught me to play
this small word had lost it's real meaning
play had become something demeaning
play along play at play up play down
play the field play favorites play upon
play it safe play for keeps play around

exercise had been my way to play
riding a bike or running away
lost all my playmates along the way
playing alone gets old after while
someone's funny face brings out a smile
play is more than the converse of work

whenever something has got you down
remember life is one big playground
think about what makes you smile
drop the other and play for awhile
play is good for the soul and for the grin
playing nice is a good way to begin

April 2016

How Many Days

"How many days until Christmas?"
Grandson Zach, six, whispered to me
"there are six more days," I answered
sighing he said, "and tomorrow,
there will be five days 'til Christmas?"
it was evening when he asked
"yes, it will be here very fast"
I did my best to persuade him

for me five days are just a flash
to Zach five days take forever
my life has been ten times longer
a wee bit more to be exact
Zach seems to have grown so quickly
learning so much in his brief time
maybe sixty-one is still young
in the big playing field of time

days move more quickly as we age
though we would like them to slow down
Zach would like his days to speed up
he wants to be bigger right now

in our own way and our own time
we must each come to grips with time
a thing finite for each of us
but much too infinite to grasp
our moments flow quickly away
into that great river

how many years of memories
can we store in a loving heart
how many days do we have left
to savor these precious memories

"Pop Pop, I am going to open some
of my presents on Christmas Eve"
"that is only five days away Zach"
Times flies except when you want it to.

December 2018

Playing with a Golden Shovel

"That enters my longhand, turns cursive,
unscarfing a zoomorphic wake, a worm of thought
I follow into the mud."
—Seamus Heaney, Viking Dublin: *Trial Pieces*

what else could always bring forth a smile that
envelops my whole being as it enters
the breach created by the front door my
grandson has just opened his longhand
still very much a work in progress turns
up or down as though alive unlike cursive
which is no longer taught in schools unscarfing
how much has been lost since the dark ages where a
computer filled an entire room zoomorphic
beast with punched cards foretelling handwriting's wake
though I digress in this tale of play a
good time is close at hand be it a worm
catching a small football or battles of
knights who fight with sticks never giving thought
to what the clock says or if it might rain I
miss an unscheduled mind happy to follow
him as his imagination leads into
places that I have long forgotten in the
mists of time as we slip away in the mud

April 2021

Skipping with Zach and the Gerrids

Memories of my youth came trickling back to me
as my grandson and I played along Herring Run
I threw the first rock into the small slightly smelly stream
Zach threw countless more stones enjoying every splash
at first he had trouble seeing the tiny water skippers
gliding magically on top of this forlorn tributary
soon he was trying to sink these slight water bugs with stones
his errant throws nearly as likely to hit land as water

"he's scared of us," he repeated after me
eyeing the small deer as it tiptoed into the underbrush
a piece of fence formed a hedge along the stream
it might have been an abandoned baby gate
taking its place here among the other waterway trash
that ended up in this hidden place during the last flood
each hole in the mesh was filled with leaves, grass, twigs, trash
like a tattered piece of parade float waiting to be assembled

finding a rare flat rock I showed him how to skip a stone
in a section of stream that could only sustain a couple skips
anxious to try for himself his stone sank on first impact
"I skipped it," he said and repeated with each sinking stone
no longer able to follow my advice about keeping dry shoes
he put his tiny sneakers partway into the water's edge
the other foot followed and sand coated the wet sneakers

soon walking became painful and he sat on my lap
on a fallen tree as I tried in vain to wipe the sand
from his not yet three year old feet using tiny damp socks
"carry me," he said and we began the long uphill walk
back to the playground in the midday heat

September 2015

Touched by Nature

Colin touched the translucent jellied mass that dangled
from the stick held by Woolly Bears teacher Miss Pam
these eggs lifted from the small pond at Oregon Ridge park
will become salamanders as the days of Spring lengthen
for four he is well-schooled in the glories of nature
monthly forays with fellow three and four year olds
they learn about pollinators reptiles amphibians birds
seeds mammals and leaves through songs snacks crafts walks

waiting and watching until the others had their turn
Colin touched the squirming tadpole
swimming in Tupperware
scooped from the leafy ooze on the pond's shallow bottom
no stranger to wiggling things he loves to hold worms
in the palm of his small hands and call them friends
chases after bunnies robins and squirrels on the lawn
stops to admire the crimson cardinal with its perfect tone
blowing downey dandelion seeds into the air never gets old
seen through fresh eyes the natural world shimmers

I thought back over fifty years to my childhood
Far away in the green hills of northwestern PA
nature was the playground in this tiny rural village
exploring deer paths in the woods behind our old home
playing in Piney Creek fifty yards from the front door
a stream full of life despite being sullied by humans
decades of strip mining had turned the rocks red
septic tank runoff dripped from steel pipes on its flanks

how many rocks were turned over in its shallows and banks
flat rocks skipped with a flick of the wrist bounced away
slim darting minnows and fat lazy chubs flowed underwater
on the surface water skippers skated to and fro like magic

crayfish propelled themselves backwards into a waiting jar
bullfrogs leaped from the shore into the safe arms of muck
mud puppies with feathery external gills hid in the shallows
they and snapping turtles he watched closely but did not touch
salamanders were the best with sleek soft skin imploring eyes

sharing in nature's splendor with the grandchildren
takes me back to a familiar place that is always new
maybe one day we can all make it back to Piney Creek
explore what now lies waiting within its ancient banks
to see it with young eyes would enliven these old eyes
may we always share our love of nature and each other

May 2019

A Smile Says It All

Though he can't talk
he says a lot
starting to walk
an expert at the crawl
he turns on wobbly legs
eyes twinkle his smile says
look at me I am walking

a master of cooing
a magnet for kisses
so much fun to hold
after he gives me the signal
big grin and outstretched arms
laughs when we rub noses
loves to nibble my fingers

he can throw a ball
climb stairs as fast as me
he's a little brother
who gets big hugs and pushed over
always dressed in a smile
and a onesie underneath
he wants whatever you have

falls asleep in the car
alert in the stroller
watches us play soccer
can't wait for him to join us
tiny fingers grab noodles and cheese
wish my aging fingers
were as agile as his

he was Robin at Halloween
big brother Batman
big sister Supergirl
laughs when I chase him
he's ticklish all over
a big tower of blocks
never stands a chance

the birthday cupcake was special
frosting oozed through fingers
the delight has been mine
watching Colin turn one
soon you will be talking
hope you always speak
with that wonderful smile

November 2015

The Quietest Day

the quietest day
is always thursday
the day after we watch
the grandkids on wednesday
from morning until evening
never-ending play fills this day

on thursday
I replay wednesday
their words reverberate
conversations serious and silly
the ever-present call to play
up down all around willy nilly

seeking and hiding inside and out
kissing boo boos cheeks heads
chasing laughter around the yard
digging worms for little hands to pet
puzzles blocks dinosaurs balls cars
keeping them upright on bikes

jumps wrestles hugs
singing silly songs
studying bugs
racing the stroller
wiping runny noses
endless calls for snacks

sticks become staffs and swords
piggyback rides irish dances
puzzles naps diaper changes
pulling on tiny socks and shoes
watching cartoons together
loving every dog bird cat

they never fail to lift my spirit
brief cries give way to smiles
every moment a time to play
the world is their playground
seeing them grow learn discover
learning much from each other

hearing them call pop pop
makes me forget
my aching back
lost in time and space
love being in this place
where so much rhymes

maybe the quietest day
is one with no play
a day when we are not needed
when no one calls out your name
a day when being is not reflected
in the smiling eyes of another

April 2017

SOMETHING ABOUT

there is something about being
with the grandkids that makes me calm
maybe it's the circle of life
maybe the things they ask of me
are things I am able to give
someone to listen to their words
toast and butter their morning bread
comfort them when they skin their knee
help them to find that missing sock
make sure they have their stuff for school
explain the meaning of a word
play monster in the swimming pool
ours is a two-way street of love

they don't ask me to change myself
with them I can be who I am
play hide and seek in the back yard
sit with them while they watch a show
fill up a glass with cold water
play nerf football in the basement
talk about heaven without fear
explain some facet of nature
deal the cards and laugh in old maid
keep ice cream on hand for dessert
wrestle playfully on the couch
walk with them to school and back home
give them a hug and kiss goodbye

February 2020

Always Be

I wish it could always be like this
Zach said around the breakfast table
you here with us, never having to die

grandma and pop pop with the grandkids
smiles waft through warm cinnamon toast
I wish it could always be like this

five, seven, nine—a moment in time
Colin, Zach, Zoe—growing up fast
you here with us, never having to die

swimming, soccer, football, gymnastics
miss Sesame Street, it's YouTube now
wish it could always be like this

roasting marshmallows over the fire
monopoly games that never end
you here with us, never having to die

heartfelt moments last a lifetime
Zach's innocent words so full of love
I wish it could always be like this
you here with us, never having to die

November 2020

FAMILY

For me, family is living history, an intersection of place and time, a moment where the poet dwells. When much of your family is far away, this history is a fragile thread that must be rediscovered, re-woven, worn often, and shared to survive.

Distant Kin

Tree roots surfaced like thoughts of distant kin
was it something someone said or did
something someone didn't say or didn't do
enjoying grandma's homemade bread with soft butter
savoring grandma's warm sugar or molasses cookies

the old barn was our favorite place to be
climbing high on straw bales or jumping in the hay
playing in the wooden bins of grain
where wheat and oats went through your hands
like hidden treasure in a pirate's cave

the smells from the old barn were exotic
spider webs dangled above liked rustic valances
walking down the hill to the soggy meadow
stepping on mounds of grass trying to keep shoes dry
in search of minnows and tadpoles and frogs

picking and eating the sweet strawberries from the patch
looking for eggs amidst the feathers and clucking
in the old chicken coop that still had a few tenants
picking up hickory nuts and black walnuts in the Fall
beneath the old trees in the lower field

walking among the vacant milking stalls thinking of cows
now departed after the fields were stripped for coal
trying to fly paper kites in the ever-present wind
chasing balls downhill with no flat ground to be found
hoarding the shiny horse chestnuts that had shed their armor

digging sassafras roots to boil for tea in grandma's kitchen
taking turns cranking the ice cream maker on the side porch
anxiously awaiting its cold creamy strawberry
savoring grandma's homemade bread with soft butter and jam
opening grandma's cookie tin to savor sugar or molasses cookies

a small gas stove with open flames in front of ceramic tiles
like an indoor campfire was the lone source of heat
we used to perch in front of it like birds on a cold morning
playing marbles on the old living room rug
conversation was our only television

the excitement of using the outdoor privy behind the house
because there was no toilet inside the aged homestead
sometimes an old Sears catalog was the only toilet paper
the boys loved the chance to pee outside in the open fields
where there were no neighbors looking out the windows

you didn't have any brothers nor we any sisters
our aunts were sisters with so much in common
we would giggle and laugh until we could hardly breath
and then a mere look would let flow tears of laughter
most of the time our fathers would be at work

we loved coming into town to play at your house
it could have been Manhattan compared to our tiny village
you had sidewalks and stores with toys and comic books

grandma lived all by herself on the farm after grandpa died
she could see no other houses from any of her windows
over the hill lay a small white church
on a plot given by our family

Grandma and Grandpa are now buried in that graveyard
along with their parents and their parents' parents
soon our parents will be gone and we—the first cousins
will be the sole keepers of these priceless memories
how did we go from being first cousins to distant kin
hope our Christmas cards find you well

March 2015

HOPE

telling someone you love
they will get better
they will be themselves again
trying to convince
both yourself and them
this is indeed true
keeping hope alive
for well over a year
joie de vie a memory
though the flame flickers
not allowing the other
to take root and grow
pushing doubt away
reassuring ever reassuring
setting time aside
repeating the prayer
as many times as it takes
until it's a part of you
til it comes true
hope is a living thing
hope is love

October 2020

Flattened Pennies

The young boys place their coins
atop the long steel rails
and then run to hide
behind stately pines
hugging close to rough bark
fingers finding sticky resin

a single headlight soon shines
grimy diesel shakes the stillness
shiny chunks of black coal
heaped in screeching cars
swaying north and south
pulled from east to west

sparks jump from steel wheels
engineer peers from open pane
the boys leap out just in time
returning the wave and smile
to the man on the caboose
as the train rounds the bend

laying claim to flattened pennies
still warm in the small palms
success in their outdoor laboratory
the earth still flat to them
stranded in a tiny village
awaiting supper's call.

March 2017

Going Home

lying still in my childhood bed
four decades after leaving home
remembering my hopes and dreams
from the sixties and seventies
wondering where the time has gone
days brimming with fun and movement

sledding down the icy hill
ice skating on the frozen pond
shooting baskets in the driveway
searching for fossils in each stone
tracking animals in the snow
gliding on clip-on roller skates

watching black and white TV shows
gluing together model cars
playing with tiny Indians
baseball cards with chewing gum
pouring over thick catalogs
candy more precious than gold

guzzling kool-aid on a hot day
looking for life in piney creek
laughter and food at grandma's house
playing catch in the backyard
swimming in the spring-filled pool
fun with cousins at reunions

loved school especially lunchtime
camaraderie of team sports
magic smell of mom's homemade pies
carried away by comic books
transistor radio in bed
glowing from a pretty girl's smile

mowing the thick sweet grass of spring
riding bikes through our small village
running on quiet country roads
hunting night crawlers after dark
playing games with little brothers
hugged by the familial bond

cherish each opportunity
to ponder life in my old room
after so many years and miles
re-playing a life now lived
nod to my old self as we pass
hopes and dreams have lives of their own

November 2018

Wooden Nickels

"don't take any wooden nickels,"
grandmother's parting words
her eldest grandson moving
far away from where she sat
rocking in an old chair
knitted blue afghan over lap
alone in an isolated farmhouse
overflowing with memories
a few visitors for warmth
she hadn't driven in years
raised seven children on the farm
during lean Depression times
grandma was the fourth of nine
with forebears in the Revolution
and the War Between the States

labor came naturally to Elsie
met grandpa at the Grange
became a wife at eighteen
double wedding with sister Bertrelle
married in her parent's home
dairy farming was in their blood
squeezed a living from rocky land
no level acre to till
everything rolled downhill
from the old gray farmhouse
flattest spot was the lonely blacktop
between Churchville and Curllsville
she sent sons overseas to war
grandma learned the hard way
"don't take any wooden nickels"

grandma made us laugh and giggle
baked the best sugar cookies
apple pies homemade bread
loved staying overnight
upstairs no lights or heat
bedpan if needs be
lots of love to warm us up
sometimes old piano sang out
when cousins converged
memories of bygone times
among the most cherished
you were my loving history
owe you a lot grandma
more than I can ever repay
don't take any wooden nickels

November 2015

THIS QUIET PLACE

Pine smoke filled the air like incense clouds
big firs who for so long had watched over
this old burial place now fed the flames
makeshift bonfire reducing them to ashes
after a spring storm had taken them down
my annual summer visit to this quiet place
changed by sounds of chainsaw and backhoe

my aunt Josephine and Uncle Jerome
first to be found starting up the grassy hill
last of our family in St. Nicholas cemetery
he drove a coal truck and she styled hair
they both loved family and laughter
long ago I served mass in this small church
an altar boy on cold winter mornings

just up the hill lie my grandparents
Jerome and Ethel and his first wife Marie
who died giving birth to uncle Richard
a second family joined the first with love
he ran a general store in Frogtown
she made beautiful wedding dresses
a grandparent now my life wanes

the plots of my great-grandparents
William and Catherine meet me
his back broken in the coal mines
a wheelchair then this spot at thirty-two
the parish, of mostly German settlers
began in 1835 only fifty years earlier
this was the domain of the Seneca

my great-great-grandparents greet me
Peter and Sarah settled here in 1850
said to have fought in the civil war
farmer township supervisor poor overseer
his obituary read like a dream
"...one of Clarion county's best citizens.
His word and work were always
in the interest of right and justice."

my great-great-great grandparents
John Henry and Margaret moved west
to also rest in these hallowed grounds
and when next I'm homeward bound
with love and care they will be found
well over two centuries they would be
one from PA the other the old country

glad to have seen these kin
their struggles still resonate
did I inherit their better traits
in this life that seems so distant
be nice to end up in this quiet place
far away from the congestion and din
an hour's walk from my family home
firmly among those who share this name

October 2015

H-O-M-E

it's going on twenty-three years now
longest I have ever lived in one place
soon it will be time to get a new roof
wish my thinning crown could be redone
it's bones much more solid than mine
water heater is on borrowed time
takes me longer to warm up too

both baby boomers this house and I
though he has about ten years on me
he's an early boomer built after WWII
I came of age during the war in Vietnam
he's sheltered lots in seven decades
I've lived in too many places to count
this old house wants me to call him home

my childhood house still feels like home
where I learned how to spell H-O-M-E
there I first learned the meaning of home
that address and phone number still ring
the other numbers have all gone silent
grew seven-teen years in the old white house
thirty-six years on it's still my parent's home

memories overflow when I return
images emerge from hibernation
hopes and wounds no longer visible
names and places long since forgotten
tastes and smells of homemade pie
turkey roasting hamburgers on the grill
home and food cannot be separated

sounds of clanking freight trains
kids at play lawnmowers distant hunters
late night snowplows coal truck brakes
we all went to the same public schools
working class people in everyday homes
called out your name at every greeting
fighting to keep the old homes running

life seemed limitless in my childhood home
life's limits now clearly within reach
thoughts migrate to the place we call home
can the heart embrace more than one home
home is the portrait we paint of ourselves
with love my wife makes this house a home
around me he creaks make yourself at home

May 2016

WAITING

she is asleep in the blue recliner
as I gaze out the hospital window
eight floors above the street
gray slate roofs slant this way and that
red brick houses and huge apartments
surrounded by a sea of green
only a few of the countless leaves
have turned from green to orange
here on this second day of autumn
yesterday my wife got a new knee
today she hopes to go back home

three long glass windows frame
the landscape of cloud sky and trees
man in yellow high on a bucket truck
works atop a brown wooden pole
clouds like unrolled cotton balls
add depth to the azure sky
cars look small as they pass below
five birds fly by and roll like jets
beeps chirp from neighboring rooms
nurses roll carts down the hallway
compression socks inhale and exhale

Evie's thirsty when she wakes up
IV lines dangle from her tiny wrist
painkillers help to ease the pain
her nurse comes in for vital signs
ninety minutes until more PT

moving a new knee is not easy
learning to walk again is hard
the body does not understand this new part
over time the two will become one
full recovery can take a year
the patient's work has just begun

September 24, 2019

A Love for All

She is the friendliest person I know
there are no strangers when Evie is near
"we're all related, we're all connected," she often crows
floats with perfect grace on the dance floor
cooking healthy recipes, her love really shows
glides upon tandem pedals over far-away roads
lots more places to smile upon, we hopefully suppose
the love of life, and generous spirit, speak to us all
of her three wonderful grandchildren, she lovingly glows
removed from time, she lives in the moment
puts heart and soul into everything, including her prose
helped , inspired, and touched too many to count
may our friendship with her be a chapter that doesn't close
let us heed Evie's call, and love each moment, one and all

January 16, 2016

HAPPY BIRTHDAY

Her beauty comes from within
lovely though she's always been
heart tender--soft as her skin
enthusiastic from way back when
makes even a stranger feel like kin
for caring, she is a ten
always there with a helping hand
positive energy is her brand
this seventy-fifth year of life
has dealt her more than enough strife
but the light still shines in her eyes
deep hazel eyes that speak volumes
of what it means to truly care
a smile is never far away
why not make a new friend today
that special beauty in living
she is so fond of giving
her beauty enveloped in love
our tandem riding--hand and glove
happy 75th Evie
you are a present to us all!

December 2020

Wearing Green

mom made sure we wore green
every St. Patrick's Day
my passion for Ireland
can surely be traced to her
you are part Irish she would say
that part has grown to this day

hitchhiked there in my twenties
lovely green fields among stone walls
welcomed me home like family
mother tongue's lilt brought a smile
beauty history rain seeped
into grassy hills and me
within ancient memory stirred

three more trips on the tandem
cycling twisty narrow lanes
searched for family tombstones
within silent Galway graveyards
grandfather Newell four greats
born in Erin 1778

best part was always the people
their warmth and caring interest
each syllable dancing forth
coaxing one to really listen
a question that always arose
"have you any Irish relatives?"

fell in love with Irish music
climbed St. Patrick's holy mountain
Croagh Patrick though not in bare feet
cozy pubs where Guinness flowed
full Irish breakfasts in B and B's
brown bread eggs bacon dark tea

have always felt at home in Eire
hope to cycle there one more time
while I still have the legs for it
getting lost on the quiet roads
asking friendly people for help
"where would you go if you were me?"

seventeenth of March each year
Winter melting into the Spring
St. Patrick must be smiling
we are all Irish on his day
thanks mom for planting this love
your Irish blessing still grows

March 2016

BITTEN

Playing in the yard on a summer day
everything is fun when you're nine
strange dog lying along the road
not far from where I'm playing
father says to stay away from stray dogs
looking sick I stay well clear of you
get away sick doggy go on home

didn't even hear a growl or paw steps
stabbing pain teeth in my leg
scream and fight to get away
crying I break free and make it to the house
mother hears my screams and runs to me
she hugs me and sends brother to the barn
father's gathering the cows for milking
comes when he hears my brother's calls
saddles up and rides for the doctor

doctor dresses my bite says I'll be alright
soon it's healing and I can play again
month later I'm screaming with pain
never had anything hurt so bad
crying is all that I can do
father and doctor gallop back for me
hold me in the wagon to the train station
leave at once for the big city

more scared than I've ever been
worried looks all around
on the train I scream in pain
they call this shaking--convulsions
takes six men to hold me down
my plea for water my screams of pain

can be heard over the roar of the train
the convulsions never stop
pain is more than I can bear
awareness slips away
losing consciousness

forty days since the bite
know you didn't mean to hurt me
sick raccoon bit you first
neither of us really had a chance
will miss you mom, dad, Ken, Bob, Don
goodbye--I love you
Russell: 9/18/1902

November 2015

Something Great

holding a great niece
and a great nephew
upon your knee
is something sweet
thirty years ago
I held their mothers
in my open arms
it was a special treat
to see our great aunts
Sister Stanislaus and Mary
staying with Grandma Reinsel
three sisters loving Scrabble
their brother Gerald my sponsor
when confirmed so long ago

Grandma Newell's siblings
brother Heber and sister Bertrelle
had very special status as well
grandma and Great-Aunt Bertrelle
had a double wedding ceremony
what questions I would love to ask
my turn of the century family
so many more greats I never got to know
now they are just names and dates on a page
alas our great aunts and uncles
fade from view as the years pass
each generation supplanted by the next

now I am the one from the last century
memories last but a lifetime
it is a special role
that of great aunt or uncle
maybe as close to royalty
as everyday family can be
I feel very lucky
with Miles, Ben, and Phoebe
we get to call each other great

April 2019

A Day in the Life

night before the big day
alarm set for three thirty
all directions followed
hope sleep will find us
we arrive in darkness
park in the tiered garage
check in and say goodbye
monitor blinks your status
patient in operating room
total left knee replacement
many years in the making
walking was difficult
riding a bike was fine
old knee will come out
metal and plastic new knee
will be in place two hours hence
my wife has been very brave
waiting is the easy part
soon the nursing will begin
what I lack in training
may I make up for in love
dream of our first bike ride
together on the tandem
four legs spinning round
down that open road
hope that ache in my left knee
soon goes away

September 2019

Waiting for Dad

lying supine
tubes sprouting
monitors flashing
fluids dripping
plugged in
looking like
an older me
worried rooms
full of waiting
human repair factory
angels in blue
taking control
new part installed
ten-year warranty
guardian angel hovering
beginning to recover
becoming unplugged
slowly walking out
a new lease on life
begins today

April 2015

Walking with My Father

We walked along the gravel road
Past the abandoned swimming pool
Long since filled in with dirt and broken concrete
Cold spring water no longer reflects the light
Or beckons swimmers

Roughly intact, the ball diamond too is silent
Stillness beneath the looming fir trees
Once laughter reigned; balls echoed from wooden bats;
Punts wobbled to earth

Further along, Piney Creek trickles
Under ancient hemlock and white pine
Red water gurgles downstream;
Old wounds from strip mining still pain me
Past the abandoned travel trailer park,
Tiny cottages have become permanent homes

Down the steep bank, across the creek,
The pond looks much the same
These still waters, under the pines, yielded bluegill
Bass, carp, crappie, catfish
Cages of barking dogs ruin the rural solitude;
We almost sneak by

White-tail deer bound across the road;
Hunting season is never far away
Wild turkeys scamper over the ditch,
Begrudgingly taking flight as we get near
Pickup driver waves hello beneath orange hunting cap;
Wheels stir up a dusty cloud

This is the walk my father did
Until he no longer could
I now inhabit his walk, alone
Recalling groundhogs scampering,
Cardinals singing, crows cawing

October 2014

AGING / ART

Aging is to become someone else within your own body. Writing about experiences has helped me to make sense of things that are in the past, but still very much alive in memory. As I grow older, nature has become even more of an inspiration for me and carpe diem ever more meaningful.

I would call myself an accidental poet. When I decided to join the Renaissance Institute, poetry was one of the few classes that had an opening. My classmates welcomed me with open hearts and beautiful poetry—thank you! Poetry helps me to express myself in ways that were beyond reach. For this, I am grateful.

Life in Small Words

We are born, grow up, grow old, and pass on.
We learn to cry, care, play, talk, smile, eat,
love, think, and sleep.

We are taught to read, write, work, pray, give, share, and save.
We are taught not to steal, cheat, lie, hit, spit, bite,
kick, or be mean.

We see, taste, smell, touch, and hear all that the world
has to share.
We dress each day for the cold, wind, rain, heat, snow, or ice.

We see red, white, black, green, brown, blue,
and gray each day.
We look to the sky, moon, stars, and sun to show
us time and place.

We run, walk, bike, jump, crawl, swim, slide, scoot,
roll, trip, and fall.
we love the bird, dog, cat, snake, deer, fish, fox,
and bug that cross our path.

We stare at the tree, stream, grass, bush, weed, and moss
that live near us.
We seek a place and role on this earth and miss the chance
when it is gone.

We start out small, get big, and then shrink if we can grow old.
We laugh when we could cry and cry when we could laugh.

We may not give small words their due,
but short words can hold their own.
We use small words to build a life
that is too big to put down in print.
We know that small words have a big role to play in life,
just like each one of us.

March 2015

(in response to a poetry assignment
to use all one-syllable words)

Antiques

fifty-seven chevy shines in the sun
used to think you were just an antique
even though we were born in the same year
suppose that makes me an antique too
your red paint sparkles under paste wax
chrome bumpers hubcaps and trim glisten
you may have a spot of rust somewhere
but your v-8 still rumbles strong and deep
how many owners have you had by now
say you don't get out of the garage much
still you really look great for your age

father time has not been as kind to me
my chassis is not what it once was
but I still have all my original parts
sun has taken its toll on my skin
aging muscles cannot lift as much
more and more names are eluding me
afraid I have lost more than a step
seems likely that you will outlast me
metal is stronger than skin and bone
fifty-seven was not famous for much
sputnik frisbee cat in the hat and you

April 2021

AGING IN PLACE

thanks to the coronavirus
cars rest in place nowhere to go
schools have been closed for many weeks
teacher now appears on a screen
students show up in tiny panes
how many more worksheets are there

businesses locked up and silent
lucky ones are working from home
others wonder what they will eat
will I be put out on the street
jobs disappear in a keystroke
we can't do without amazon

face masks have become essential
are scarce and essential the same
hand washing is now like breathing
how many more days can I stretch
all of the food we have on hand
no use talking toilet paper

winter lockdown would be much worse
darkness inside the soul and out
cycling and walking is my tonic
moving amongst the budding trees
spring and easter arrived early
praying for a resurrection

neighbors cast such wary glances
six feet apart is now the rule
it's such a long way from grandkids

TV news updates the death toll
days of quarantine tick away
our lives remain largely on hold

the earth has always aged in place
rocks measure time so silently
trees mutely add a ring each year
nature seems immune to this plague
would that we spoke the same language
now we might listen and take heed

April 2020

Amalgam

My teeth are cracking
weakened by age
and the decades
of countless bites
untold clenches
old silver fillings
shine out at me
when I peer
open-mouthed
into the mirror

nothing is forever
things are easy to take
for granted until
they begin to ache
like a broken heart
full of holes
where none
should be
making it hard
to partake
of life

amalgam
does not live.

June 2017

GRAVITAS

never thought that much about gravity
other forces had a better hold on me
or so I believed--until recently
just the other day read that we
are all the "children of gravity"
knew it caused the tidal sea
studied Newton's apple tree
being related to gravity
was not my kind of family

mostly gravity was benign to me
this year will mark fifty years
since the Apollo 11 astronauts
took those big steps on the moon
making me wish I wore a spacesuit
and could spring up with each step
exploiting the moon's weak gravity
alas all things with mass or energy
must heed the laws of gravity—even me

regrettably as we grow old
our body succumbs to gravity
skin and organs begin to sag
varicose veins and failing hearts
gravity pulls us older folks down
now we have something else to blame
when our back aches and arthritis strikes
if it weren't for that pesky gravity
I would look and feel a lot younger

April 2019

Given Time

Given time anything can break
from families to fixtures to friendships
fences to furniture to faith
from truth to trees to trust
teeth to toys to tools
from lives to locks to looks
love to lawnmowers to lollipops
from hearts to homes to hope
habitat to happiness to habit
from promises to plumbing to pavement
pencils to peace to policies
from windows to waistlines to wooing
wings to wainscoting to whimsy

from noses to necklaces to nerves
appointments to allegiances to appetites
from shoelaces to spirits to spokes
silence to shadows to skin
from driveways to diets to doorknobs
eyeglasses to enthusiasm to eardrums
from careers to cookies to clouds
vows to voices to virility
from memories to mirrors to minds
baskets to bones to bank accounts
from roles to rivalries to routes
records to riverbanks to rocks

Given time, will, and love
many things can be broken
from fear to fallacy to folderol
hatred to hegemony to histrionics

from poverty to plagiarism to pollution
greed to gangs to grudges
from spying to stereotypes to superficiality
sadness to sensibilities to secrets
from corruption to corporate welfare to chaos
cruelty to crying to climate change

from loneliness to litigation to lying
limits to lethargy to laws
from walls to warmongering to waste
violence to vendettas to vitriol
from disease to disuse to dogma
bullies to bastions to bogymen
from anxiety to addiction to apathy
harnesses to hairstyles to halitosis
from ignorance to isolation to ignominy
expectations to euphemisms to eulogies

Given time much is possible.

March 2017

Communion

we wait in the rain
long line loops around
this state cathedral
hints of roman times
though today's service
is a noble one

strangers gathering
with one goal in mind
voices low muffled
behind varied masks
young seniors teachers
front line workers too

few common causes
leave us divided
virus has triumphed
for over a year
its tiny minions
vanish in thin air

soon we move inside
out of the cold rain
into the bowels
troops oversee the line
mood is positive
our mission is clear

it is up on high
beside sky boxes
shoulder uncovered
each receives a jab
we come together
for the good of us all

March 2021

IDENTITY

age
    ancestry
        accent
            bumper stickers
                baseball caps
                    country
                        culture
                            community
                            communication device
                      diet
                flag
            gender
        heritage
    hobbies
holidays
    jewelry
        language
            marital status
                modes of travel
                    music
                        news outlets
                            occupation
                        operating system
                  postal code
              political party
            pets
        philosophy
    residence
schools attended
      social networks
        state
            sports teams
            skin color

                    sexual orientation
                         school district
                              tax bracket
                                traditions
                            television shows
                              t-shirts
                    vehicles
                 websites
            our human family just keeps growing
    so do the ways of telling us apart

October 2017

INDEBTED TO PHEIDIPPIDES

ran twenty-five miles from Marathon to Athens
through unkind terrain carrying news of a Greek
victory over Persia in the battle of Marathon
he breathed his last saying "joy to you we've won"
at forty Pheidippides died a hero after his epic run
ran my first marathon nearly 2500 years later
at nineteen I "hit the wall" after twenty miles on Presque Isle

started running in the backyard and loved every stride
seem to have my father's legs they never let me down
running through recess fields forests courts tracks and roads
running under arcing touchdown passes as time stood still
running saved me after a tough season of college football
Shorter's Olympic win in '72 made the distance golden
dreams of the Boston marathon lit a new flame within

big jump from the quarter mile in track to twenty-six
lonely miles on the road but the test was romantic
long distance running suited my reticent nature
plenty of room to run despite the dogs and coal trucks
up and down the back roads of rural PA
ran one-hundred and five miles one week in training
ate enough to break even the calories were raining

took eight years and five marathons to qualify
Boston's standard was 26.2 under 2 hours 50 minutes
my dream was fulfilled at the Marine Corps marathon
had my heart broken at Heartbreak Hill in Boston
the famous April race a stern test in so many ways
for a schoolteacher running through winter's worst
Boston's finishing medal a bittersweet last hurrah

I dearly miss running
had to give it up ten years ago
lower back could take no more
now I only run after the grandkids
we play tag or race in the backyard
"run Pop Pop run" they often cheer
next day my back usually jeers

miss that runner's high and discovering
something new around the next bend
thanks Pheidippides for your great pace
walking now to life's finish line
a marathon hasn't really begun
until twenty miles have been run
will I feel joy when I finish this race

March 2016

FRANK'S GIFT

When Frank smiled that big smile
you couldn't help but beam
from both inside and out
this happened quite often
because Frank loved to smile
he was quick with a joke too
and always made you laugh
swift on their tandem bike
Kathy and Frank sailed along
the miles flew by with Frank
fun lay around each bend
Frank just made everything fun

always ready to play
the life of the party
great on any dance floor
quick to offer a toast
his booming laugh so fun
his handshake filled with love
a twinkle in his eye
his ever-present smile
his sense of joy and wonder
Frank made life a party

always a family man
built a tree house with love
Natalie and Jacob
grandchildren in his heart
the Spring Fling his platform
Kathy by his side
Becky, Larry and the kids
hundreds of smiling cyclists
Frank made good things happen

an honor to know him
we will always miss Frank
he left us far too soon
he was a gift to all
a gentle man of fun
Frank's smile lives on in us
he will stay in our hearts
his smile, his spark, his spirit.

Michael & Evie Reinsel, February 2019

AMONG FRIENDS

piano pounds out the ceaseless progress of time
walking beside the white dog on a majestic lawn
for six years we have been guests at Downton
we have shared in your good times and bad
you have made our mother tongue seem royal
handsome tweed suits beside elegant silk dresses
love your library even if I never opened a book
gave up hunting long ago but would join yours
though not by blood downstairs is family too
you reveal nobility in your lives of service
the bustling kitchen is the warmest room
will miss dining with you at the long table
but as Mrs. Hughes said, "no life is carefree"
regardless of rank the essential title is friend

March 2016

ONLY

I am an only child
not that I ever wanted
to be anything else
what choice does one
have in such matters
you might as well wish
for blue eyes instead of brown
like everything else
only has its ups and downs

affections never to be shared
playing catch with yourself
no hand-me-down shirts shoes
experiences that are yours alone
never called by another's name
losses shouldered only by you
I never asked to be an only child
though it might be good practice
after all we die alone

April 2017

FOUND A PEN

found a pen on my walk today
on the way to life-long learning
pass it by then double back
who knows why
mostly let fallen pens lie

gloved-hand reaches down
rescue it from the sidewalk
white cylinder with blue top
holiday inn express it reads
no bare skin to see if it writes

how did it get here
whose hand held it
where has it been
what has it written
what stories can it tell

inside with notebook open
smile as ink flows freely
take notes on birding, poetry
stories of katherine anne porter
what other things will it bring to life

maybe it will be my muse
it has written these lines
what more does it have to say
found a pen today
or maybe it found me

February 2019

Everyday Artists

six foot long Lusitania made from matchsticks
life-size bearded man sculpted with colored wire
robots constructed from old vacuum cleaners
Stegosaurus built from a thousand discarded items
large oil painting depicting the looming apocalypse
window screens painted with pastoral scenes
hundreds of mirrors hide an ordinary car
labors of love that devour days, years, decades, lives

personal art from unconventional artists
discarded objects become something beautiful
these everyday artists cry out to us
repent, forgive, love one another, believe

they have learned the hard way
speaking through their art
each abode an art gallery
every day an occasion to create

I feel uncreative pondering this fanciful art
but it awakens a will to create
fanning an ember deep within
wanting to catch fire and become real

these masterpieces whisper
create something
make yourself smile
never stop

February 2016

This poem was inspired by a visit to the American Visionary Arts Museum in Baltimore.

I Should Have Been

sitting down with paper and pen
trying to come up with a line of text
each word fitting perfectly to the next
like puzzle pieces when new
painting a picture with words
finding a rhyme for the end of a line
an onomatopoeia when it's time
a metaphor would also be fine

relating a feeling or experience
to a reader's heart and five senses
an essence in just a few sentences
first draft is a bit disheveled
cutting and sanding each stanza
third time through it calls to you
where did I put that thesaurus
too much polish makes it porous

instead of enjoying the sublime weather
feeling guilty for time spent outdoors
in the silky air with a feathery breeze
admiring once forgotten plants and trees
riding the tandem over hill and gorge
amidst the silent majesty of Gettysburg
the tulips and tourists of Sherwood Garden
past giraffes feeding in Druid Hill Park

in place of playing grandchildren's games
singing silly songs to make them giggle
watching cartoons that make them wriggle
trimming tall hedges along our front porch

now the sun shines no need for a torch
palling with Dickens' David Copperfield
immersed in epic poems by Polish poets
I should have been writing a poem

April 2016

THE HARDEST PART

is writing down the first line
a poem doesn't have to rhyme
punctuation capitalization grammar
these conventions are optional too

poems are not just written
by cloistered spinsters
or old men hidden
behind long white beards
though both personas
have their merits

poetry can be
written and spoken
by you and by me
the only necessary
is having something to say
an emotion clawing its way
into the dim light of day
poetry is less work
and more play

poets write poetry
to make themselves smile
poetry is darning
that hole in your spirit
a poem tells a story
worth remembering

poets don't anticipate
being famous or paid
the cause for a big parade

poetry is written
mostly for ourselves
a dialogue with being
something loved or lost
poets bring life to words

poetry is shaking hands
with the moment
sharing a laugh or a cry
always wondering why
setting life to verse
enriched by the process

poets aren't all dead
we are all poets
waiting to be read
the hardest part
is writing down the first line

March 2017

If Only I Had Known

The title **poet** rings of magic
pulling words out of thin air
making images come to life

didn't know of any poets
in the time and at the place
where my identity took shape

can't remember writing a poem
we must have studied a few?
when I was a lad in school

poetry was something antique
found only on dusty shelves
written by long-dead souls

the sonnets of Shakespeare
Longfellow's Paul Revere
Frost's less taken road

making every line end in rhyme
seemed to take no end of time
for bookworms that was fine

why stay inside and play with words
when outside there are balls bows
bikes slingshots knives rods snow

poetry is written to recite
my shyness spoke by listening
poetry brings emotions to light
my feelings were tamped down tight

in retirement I went back to school
signed up late all the classes full
what harm could befall me in poetry

if only I had known
everyone has a ***poet***
hiding inside wanting to share
secret thoughts only we can bare
like E. Dickinson's buzzing fly
if only I had known--Robert Bly.

February 2017

Living in the Shadow

the towering hemlocks are sentient
watching over the town cemetery
more than two centuries in the making
tucked on a hillside above the village
surrounded by trees and moss-laden grass
at the end of a road where no one goes
some few but storied residents lie still

the past is present in this place
thoughts of lives gone by permeate
with each step familiar names unravel
most long dead but some I once knew
craig etched in granite stands tall
my quest for a civil war relation
resting in the shadow of the pines

colonel calvin craig lies here
a relative on my grandfather's side
shiver as I stand next to his grave
so much left unsaid on the plain headstone
tell me of your courage at gettysburg
yorktown petersburg bull run wilderness
commanding the PA hundred and fifth

my shadow moves among the weathered gravestones
small medallions mark the veteran's graves
some fought in 1812 others the civil war
heroes sleep here in splendid quietude
in this place rests colonel calvin craig
he pledged and gave his life for the union
in the end connections are all we have

August 2021

The Poet Within

writes sonnets in all she does
rhymes with everyone she meets
each move brings meaning to life
her meter is just being
each day a poem complete
each act a stanza of love
experience her teacher
she instructs by words and deeds

she writes love poems to all
each line is filled with being
she chooses her words with care
her poems leave me smiling
always sees the big picture
knows we are all related
wants to rewrite our past wrongs
writes in the language of love

makes my poems come to life
edits my work in progress
sticks by me when I don't rhyme
helps me to write adventures
she champions my poetry
only she can get me to read
shares memories words don't know
saved the best decades for me

her body is her temple
healthy foods her alphabet
exercise her perfect verse
recites wisdom from her heart

inspires me to be better
a friend to all that she meets
gives more love than I deserve

the poet within loves me
we share a poem called life
the stanzas are uneven
each line doesn't always rhyme
the meter is one of love
I would be lost beyond words
without the poet within

December 2018

The Poet Next Door

the poet next door
moves me with her words
painting life on lines
quiet in her ways
careful not to show
this alter ego

the poet next door
writes of loss and pain
life in her garden
beauty and dying
smiles when we meet
inspires me to write

the poet next door
rakes the stuff of life
keeping what she finds
when time becomes words
not to be erased
but often rearranged

the poet next door
never seems to age
breathing in haiku
exhaling small worlds
of meter and rhyme
before time expires

the poet next door
always has a poem

September 2018

Playing Catch

played catch with my grandson yesterday
big smile and small voice erasing my years
never played catch with my grandfathers
they died before I was old enough to ask
born in the late nineteenth century
there was always some work to be done
on the farms when they came of age
plowing planting milking making hay
memories of my grandfathers are lost

I think they would have played catch
if only I had the chance to ask
if only they were younger then
not so tired from a life of work
if only it was just the two of us
we could have made a ball from twine
laugh at wayward throws dropped balls
tell me stories from their childhood
family resemblances coming to life

pops throw the ball real high comes the cry
wish they could see me with Colin and Zach
grandfathers and grandsons are made for each other

June 2021

In Another Life

(for Dan Maguire)

in another life
i imagine us as fellow priests
we hear each other's confessions
do our best to heal co-sinners
in a world that seems not to care
speak latin as our second tongue
sometimes slip into pig latin
muse on the knights templar
debate ancient papal bulls
you recite the baltimore catechism
have you ever forgotten anything

in another life
i imagine us as professors
words on the page our passion
popular culture an avocation
long walks in the countryside
never at a loss for words
stop for pints in a country pub
your laughter a magnet for all
on the evening walk home
we break into song
relics from warren zevon
as always you in fine voice
ever a twinkle in your eye

in another life
you are the master poet
a wordsmith beyond reproach
i am only a beginner
you deliver indelible lines
joyce and heaney never far away

before recalling hundred yard sprints
fast and graceful like your poems
those races ended in victory
unlike the lovely sad finishes
that often close your best verse
philly is your middle-earth
love gone astray a rich loam
you uncover with keen eyes
ever hopeful you find the best
in what others recite to you
be yourself you seem to say

in another life
i would have met you sooner

November 2020

About the Author

MICHAEL REINSEL taught high school business for 32 years in Oregon and Maryland. He grew up in a small village in Clarion County, PA, where he earned his bachelor's degree. A master's degree from Oregon State University and Ph.D. from the University of Maryland followed. Sports were his first love and all things outdoors. His hobbies include cycling, mostly on a tandem bike with his wife Evie, fun of all sorts with their three grandchildren, travel, music, and reading classic fiction. Michael has been a student at The Renaissance Institute—a lifelong learning community in Baltimore—for the past 7 years.

www.ingramcontent.com/pod-product-compliance
Lightning Source LLC
Chambersburg PA
CBHW020532080526
44583CB00013B/827